Made in the USA
Columbia, SC
03 November 2020

Jonah

An Illustrated Hebrew Reader's Edition

Jesse R. Scheumann and Merissa Scheumann

Illustrated by Christine Lynn Hiegel

HA'ARETS

HEBREW & ARAMAIC ACCESSIBLE RESOURCES
FOR EXEGETICAL AND THEOLOGICAL STUDIES

SERIES EDITORS

TRAVIS WEST   JESSE R. SCHEUMANN

GlossaHouse
Wilmore, KY
www.glossahouse.com

HA'ARETS

The Hebrew word הָאָרֶץ means "the earth, the land." It refers to the entirety of the physical world we see and touch and live upon. It is the creation of God, a gift for sustaining life and gladdening the heart, and it is the primary space of God's self-revelation. The HA'ARETS series—Hebrew & Aramaic Accessible Resources for Exegetical and Theological Studies—is an innovative curriculum suite offering resources that participate in the life-giving richness of הָאָרֶץ. The suite offers affordable and innovative print and electronic resources including grammars, readers, specialized studies, and other exegetical materials that encourage and foster the exegetical use of biblical Hebrew and Aramaic for the world and the global church.

Preface

This book illustrates every phrase from the book of Jonah. The goal was to include enough details in the images for each Hebrew word to have a picture referent on the page.

Our method divided the Hebrew text into two categories: narrative and reported speech. Narrative text is depicted in black-and-white illustrations, and the corresponding Hebrew is placed in grey text boxes. Reported speech is depicted in full-color illustrations within "speech bubbles," and the corresponding Hebrew is placed in salmon-colored text boxes.

The text boxes are strictly arranged from top to bottom on the page, and generally should be read from right to left. Whenever two text boxes are on the same level, the text box on the right should be read first. All of the illustrations are arranged so that the character orientation and "movement" flow from right to left.

We laid out the Hebrew text as a reader's edition with less-frequent vocabulary footnoted on the bottom of each page. As a complement to the *Picture Hebrew Flashcards*, this book footnotes non-verbs that occur fewer than 100 times in the Hebrew Bible, and verbs with a root that occurs fewer than 100 times. All verbs are listed in the 3ms qatal (perfect) form with a code that indicates the binyan (stem). Glosses are adapted from HALOT. There is a Hebrew-English dictionary at the back of the book for all non-footnoted words.

In general, the illustrations depict a natural interpretation of the text, especially by not taking idioms literally. But Jonah's colorful descriptions of his underwater plight in chapter two are captured in a literal word-to-image manner. Part of this is for pedagogical purposes to teach the infrequent vocabulary used in the poem. The other reason is keeping in line with the nature of poetry, where an author often uses strange imagery to jolt the audience into thinking about a situation with a deeper meaning. We try to capture this imagery.

For about a dozen scenes, it might be a hard to see what we intended to illustrate, even after learning all of the vocabulary. A few of these illustrations are necessarily interpretive. These scenes are explained on a page just before the dictionary at the end of the book.

We, Jesse and Merissa, decided how to illustrate the Hebrew text on every page. Our artist, Christine Hiegel, brought this design to life with her paintings. Her work has made this a beautiful, effective learning resource. Along the way, we received valuable feedback from Brian Schultz, Ben Kantor, Scott McQuinn, Nate Sheppard, and our 2016–2017 Hebrew students. If there is any lack in this book, the blame rests solely at our feet. For more resources on internalizing the language of Scripture, visit www.glossahouse.com.

- Jesse and Merissa

וַיָּ֤קׇם יוֹנָה֙ לִבְרֹ֙חַ֙[1] תַּרְשִׁ֔ישָׁה מִלִּפְנֵ֖י יְהֹוָ֑ה וַיֵּ֣רֶד יָפ֗וֹ

וַיִּמְצָ֣א אׇנִיָּ֣ה[2] ׀ בָּ֣אָה תַרְשִׁ֗ישׁ

וַיִּתֵּ֤ן שְׂכָרָהּ֙[3]

[1] בָּרַח Q: run away, flee [2] אׇנִיָּה ship [3] שָׂכָר payment, fee

וַיהוָ֗ה הֵטִ֤יל¹ רֽוּחַ־גְּדוֹלָה֙ אֶל־הַיָּ֔ם

וַיְהִ֥י סַֽעַר²־גָּד֖וֹל בַּיָּ֑ם

וְהָ֣אֳנִיָּ֔ה³ חִשְּׁבָ֖ה לְהִשָּׁבֵֽר:

1:4

¹הֵטִיל HI: throw far, hurl ²סַ֫עַר storm, heavy gale ³אֳנִיָּה ship

וַיִּֽירְא֣וּ הַמַּלָּחִים֮¹

וַֽיִּזְעֲקוּ֮² אִ֤ישׁ אֶל־אֱלֹהָיו֒

וַיָּטִ֜לוּ³ אֶת־הַכֵּלִ֨ים אֲשֶׁ֤ר בָּֽאֳנִיָּה֙⁴ אֶל־הַיָּ֔ם לְהָקֵ֥ל⁵ מֵֽעֲלֵיהֶ֑ם

1:5a

¹מַלָּח sailor ²זָעַק Q: shout, cry out ³הֵטִיל HI: throw far, hurl ⁴אֳנִיָּה ship ⁵הֵקֵל HI: lighten

וְיוֹנָה יָרַד֙ אֶל־יַרְכְּתֵ֣י¹ הַסְּפִינָ֔ה²

וַיִּשְׁכַּ֖ב

וַיֵּרָדַֽם:³

¹יַרְכָּה rear, far part ²סְפִינָה ship (with a deck) ³נִרְדַּם NI: be fast asleep, sleep deeply

1:6

¹רַב חֹבֵל captain ²נִרְדָּם NI: be fast asleep ³אוּלַי maybe, perhaps ⁴הִתְעַשֵּׁת HTP: consider, take notice

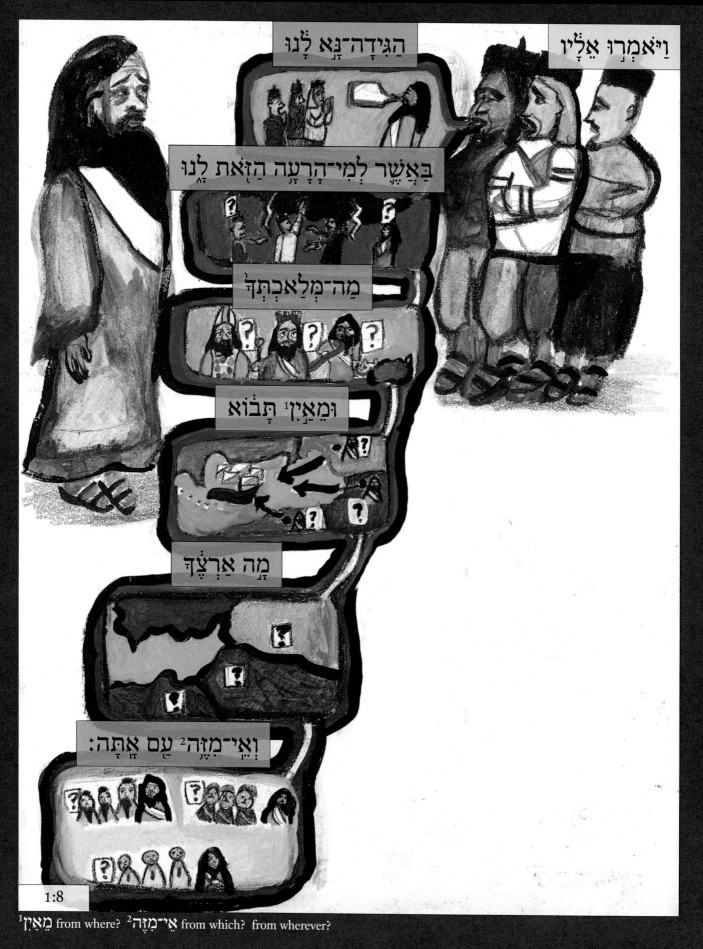

מֵאַ֫יִן[1] from where? אֵי־מִזֶּה[2] from which? from wherever?

עִבְרִי a Hebrew ²יַבָּשָׁה dry land

¹יְרֵאָה fear ²בָּרַח Q: run away, flee

וַיֹּאמְר֤וּ אֵלָיו֙ מַה־נַּ֣עֲשֶׂה לָּ֔ךְ

וְיִשְׁתֹּ֥ק¹ הַיָּ֖ם מֵֽעָלֵ֑ינוּ

כִּ֥י הַיָּ֖ם הוֹלֵ֥ךְ וְסֹעֵֽר²

1:11

¹שָׁתַק Q: be silent ²סָעַר Q: be stormy

וַיֹּאמֶר אֲלֵיהֶם

שָׂאוּנִי

וַהֲטִילֻנִי[1] אֶל־הַיָּם

וְיִשְׁתֹּק[2] הַיָּם מֵעֲלֵיכֶם

כִּי יוֹדֵעַ אָנִי
כִּי בְשֶׁלִּי הַסַּעַר[3] הַגָּדוֹל הַזֶּה עֲלֵיכֶם׃

1:12

הֵטִיל[1] HI: throw far, hurl שָׁתַק[2] Q: be silent סַעַר[3] storm, heavy gale

וַיַּחְתְּרוּ[1] הָאֲנָשִׁים
לְהָשִׁיב אֶל־הַיַּבָּשָׁה[2]

וְלֹא יָכֹלוּ
כִּי הַיָּם הוֹלֵךְ וְסֹעֵר[3] עֲלֵיהֶם:

1:13

חָתַר[1] Q: dig, row   יַבָּשָׁה[2] dry land   סָעַר[3] Q: be stormy

וַיִּקְרְא֣וּ אֶל־יְהֹוָ֗ה וַיֹּאמְר֞וּ

אָנָּ֤ה¹ יְהֹוָה֙ אַל־נָ֣א נֹאבְדָ֗ה בְּנֶ֙פֶשׁ֙ הָאִ֣ישׁ הַזֶּ֔ה

1:14a

¹אָנָּ֤ה please

1:14b

נָקִיא[1] innocent, clean חָפֵץ[2] Q: take pleasure in, want

וַיִּשְׂאוּ֙ אֶת־יוֹנָ֔ה

וַיְטִלֻ֖הוּ[1] אֶל־הַיָּ֑ם

וַיַּעֲמֹ֥ד הַיָּ֖ם מִזַּעְפּֽוֹ[2]:

1:15

[1]הֵטִיל HI: throw far, hurl [2]זָעַף Q: rage

וַיִּֽירְא֧וּ הָאֲנָשִׁ֛ים יִרְאָ֥ה¹ גְדוֹלָ֖ה אֶת־יְהוָֹ֑ה

וַיִּזְבְּחוּ־זֶ֙בַח֙ לַֽיהוָֹ֔ה

וַיִּדְּר֖וּ² נְדָרִֽים³׃

1:16

¹ יִרְאָה fear ² נָדַר Q: vow, solemnly promise ³ נֶדֶר vow

וַיְמַן֩ יְהוָ֨ה דָּ֤ג גָּדוֹל֙ לִבְלֹ֣עַ אֶת־יוֹנָ֔ה

וַיְהִ֤י יוֹנָה֙ בִּמְעֵ֣י הַדָּ֔ג שְׁלֹשָׁ֥ה יָמִ֖ים וּשְׁלֹשָׁ֥ה לֵילֽוֹת׃

2:1

¹ מָנָה PI: appoint ² דָּג fish ³ בָּלַע Q: swallow ⁴ מֵעַיִם inner organs, intestines

וַיִּתְפַּלֵּל[1] יוֹנָה אֶל־יְהוָה אֱלֹהָיו מִמְּעֵי[2] הַדָּגָה:[3] וַיֹּאמֶר

קָרָאתִי מִצָּרָה[4] לִי אֶל־יְהוָה

וַיַּעֲנֵנִי

מִבֶּטֶן[5] שְׁאוֹל[6] שִׁוַּעְתִּי[7]

שָׁמַעְתָּ קוֹלִי:

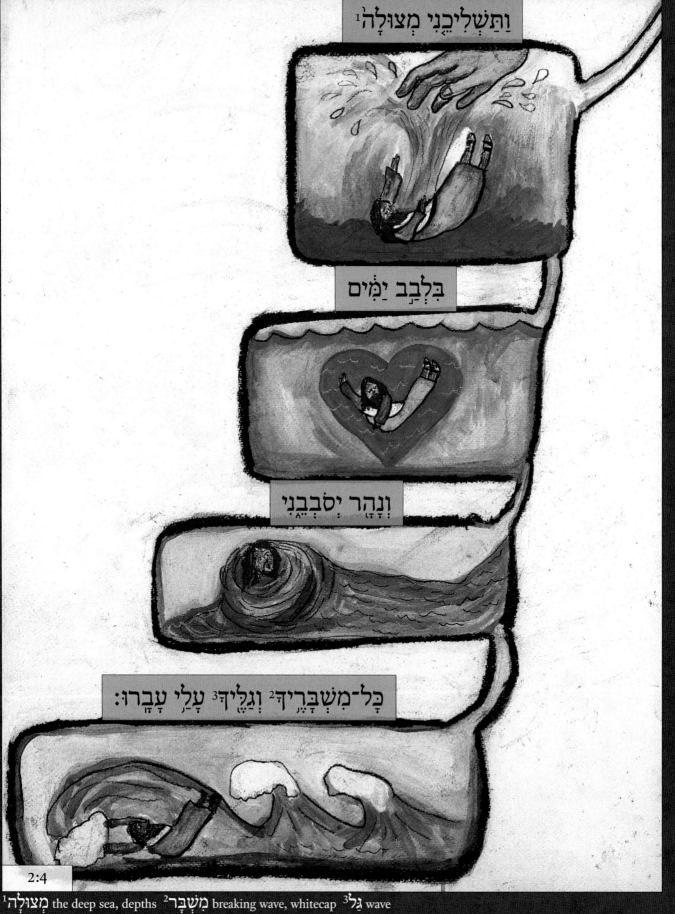

וַתַּשְׁלִיכֵנִי מְצוּלָה[1]

בִּלְבַב יַמִּ֒ים

וְנָהָר יְסֹבְבֵנִי

כָּל־מִשְׁבָּרֶיךָ[2] וְגַלֶּיךָ[3] עָלַי עָבָרוּ׃

2:4

[1] מְצוּלָה the deep sea, depths [2] מִשְׁבָּר breaking wave, whitecap [3] גַּל wave

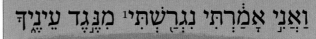

וַאֲנִי אָמַרְתִּי נִגְרַשְׁתִּי¹ מִנֶּגֶד עֵינֶיךָ

אַךְ אוֹסִיף לְהַבִּיט² אֶל־הֵיכַל³ קָדְשֶׁךָ׃

אֲפָפוּנִי⁴ מַיִם עַד־נֶפֶשׁ

תְּהוֹם⁵ יְסֹבְבֵנִי סוּף⁶ חָבוּשׁ⁷ לְרֹאשִׁי׃

2:5-6

¹נִגְרַשׁ NI: be cast out ²הַבִּיט HI: gaze ³הֵיכָל temple ⁴אָפַף Q: engulf ⁵תְּהוֹם primeval ocean ⁶סוּף reeds ⁷חָבֻשׁ Q: wrap

לְקִצְבֵי¹ הָרִים֙ יָרַ֔דְתִּי

הָאָ֛רֶץ בְּרִחֶ֥יהָ² בַעֲדִ֖י לְעוֹלָ֑ם

וַתַּ֧עַל מִשַּׁ֛חַת³ חַיַּ֖י יְהוָ֥ה אֱלֹהָֽי׃

2:7

קֶ֫צֶב¹ extremity, base ²בְּרִיחַ bar ³שַׁחַת pit, grave

בְּהִתְעַטֵּף[1] עָלַי נַפְשִׁי
אֶת־יְהוָה זָכָרְתִּי

וַתָּבוֹא אֵלֶיךָ תְּפִלָּתִי[2]
אֶל־הֵיכַל[3] קָדְשֶׁךָ:

2:8

[1] הִתְעַטֵּף HTP: feel weak, be faint   [2] תְּפִלָּה prayer   [3] הֵיכָל temple

מְשַׁמְּרִים הַבְלֵי־שָׁוְא[1][2] חַסְדָּם יַעֲזֹבוּ:

וַאֲנִי בְּקוֹל תּוֹדָה[3] אֶזְבְּחָה־לָּךְ

אֲשֶׁר נָדַרְתִּי[4] אֲשַׁלֵּמָה

2:9–10a

[1] הֶבֶל breath, vapor [2] שָׁוְא worthlessness [3] תּוֹדָה thanksgiving [4] נָדַר Q: vow, solemnly promise

יְשׁוּעָ֛תָה¹ לַיהוָ֖ה׃

וַיֹּ֥אמֶר יְהוָ֖ה לַדָּ֑ג²
וַיָּקֵ֥א³ אֶת־יוֹנָ֖ה אֶל־הַיַּבָּשָֽׁה⁴׃

¹יְשׁוּעָה help, salvation ²דָּג fish ³הֵקִיא HI: vomit, throw up ⁴יַבָּשָׁה dry land

¹קְרִיאָה proclamation, message

וַיָּ֣קׇם יוֹנָ֗ה
וַיֵּ֛לֶךְ אֶל־נִֽינְוֵ֖ה כִּדְבַ֣ר יְהֹוָ֑ה

נינוה

וְנִֽינְוֵ֗ה הָיְתָ֤ה עִיר־גְּדוֹלָה֙ לֵֽאלֹהִ֔ים מַהֲלַ֖ךְ¹ שְׁלֹ֥שֶׁת יָמִֽים׃

¹מַהֲלַךְ journey, walk

וַיָּחֶל יוֹנָה֙ לָב֣וֹא בָעִ֔יר מַהֲלַ֖ךְ¹ י֣וֹם אֶחָ֑ד

וַיִּקְרָא֙ וַיֹּאמַ֔ר

ע֛וֹד אַרְבָּעִ֥ים י֖וֹם וְנִֽינְוֵ֥ה נֶהְפָּֽכֶת²:

¹מַהֲלַךְ journey, walk ²נֶהְפָּכֶת NI: be overturned

וַיַּאֲמִ֥ינוּ¹ אַנְשֵׁ֥י נִֽינְוֵ֖ה בֵּֽאלֹהִ֑ים

וַיִּקְרְאוּ־צוֹם²

וַיִּלְבְּשׁ֣וּ שַׂקִּ֔ים³ מִגְּדוֹלָ֖ם וְעַד־קְטַנָּֽם׃⁴

3:5

¹הֶאֱמִין HI: trust, believe ²צוֹם fast, period of fasting ³שַׂק sackcloth, burlap ⁴קָטֹן small

וַיִּגַּע הַדָּבָר אֶל־מֶלֶךְ נִינְוֵה

וַיָּקָם מִכִּסְאֹו
וַיַּעֲבֵר אַדַּרְתֹּו[1] מֵעָלָיו

וַיְכַס שַׂק[2]
וַיֵּשֶׁב עַל־הָאֵפֶר[3]:

3:6

[1] אַדֶּרֶת robe [2] שַׂק sackcloth, burlap [3] אֵפֶר ashes

וַיַּזְעֵק֙¹ וַיֹּ֙אמֶר֙ בְּנִֽינְוֵ֔ה

מִטַּ֧עַם² הַמֶּ֛לֶךְ וּגְדֹלָ֖יו לֵאמֹ֑ר

הָֽאָדָ֣ם וְהַבְּהֵמָ֗ה הַבָּקָ֤ר וְהַצֹּ֙אן֙

אַֽל־יִטְעֲמוּ֙³ מְא֔וּמָה⁴ אַ֨ל־יִרְע֔וּ וּמַ֖יִם אַל־יִשְׁתּֽוּ׃

3:7

הַזְעִיק¹ HI: make a proclamation, summon ²טַעַם taste; decree ³טַעַם Q: taste ⁴מְאוּמָה anything

וַיִּתְכַּסּוּ שַׂקִּים¹ הָאָדָם וְהַבְּהֵמָה

וַיִּקְרְאוּ אֶל־אֱלֹהִים בְּחָזְקָה²

וַיָּשֻׁבוּ אִישׁ מִדַּרְכּוֹ הָרָעָה וּמִן־הֶחָמָס³ אֲשֶׁר בְּכַפֵּיהֶם:

3:8

¹שַׂק sackcloth, burlap ²חָזְקָה strength ³חָמָס violence

מִי־יוֹדֵעַ

יָשׁוּב וְנִחַם הָאֱלֹהִים

וְשָׁב מֵחֲרוֹן אַפּוֹ

וְלֹא נֹאבֵד:

3:9

וַיַּ֤רְא הָֽאֱלֹהִים֙ אֶֽת־מַ֣עֲשֵׂיהֶ֔ם כִּי־שָׁ֖בוּ מִדַּרְכָּ֣ם הָֽרָעָ֑ה

וַיִּנָּ֣חֶם הָאֱלֹהִ֗ים עַל־הָרָעָ֛ה אֲשֶׁר־דִּבֶּ֥ר לַעֲשׂוֹת־לָהֶ֖ם

וְלֹ֥א עָשָֽׂה׃

3:10

 חָרָה [1] Q: become hot, be kindled הִתְפַּלֵּל [2] HTP: pray אָנָּה [3] please

עַל־כֵּן קִדַּמְתִּי[1] לִבְרֹחַ[2] תַּרְשִׁישָׁה כִּי יָדַעְתִּי

נִינְוֵה

תַּרְשִׁישׁ

כִּי אַתָּה אֵל־חַנּוּן[3]

וְרַחוּם[4]

אֶרֶךְ[5] אַפַּיִם

וְרַב־חֶסֶד

586 B.C. 770 B.C. 1446 B.C.

וְנִחָם עַל־הָרָעָה:

4:2b

[1] קדם PI: go ahead, do early [2] ברח Q: run away [3] חנון gracious, merciful [4] רחום tender, compassionate [5] ארך length

וַיֵּצֵא יוֹנָה֙ מִן־הָעִ֔יר

וַיֵּ֥שֶׁב מִקֶּ֖דֶם¹ לָעִ֑יר

וַיַּ֩עַשׂ֩ לוֹ֨ שָׁ֜ם סֻכָּ֗ה²

וַיֵּ֣שֶׁב תַּחְתֶּ֘יהָ֮ בַּצֵּל֒³
עַ֚ד אֲשֶׁ֣ר יִרְאֶ֔ה מַה־יִּהְיֶ֖ה בָּעִֽיר׃

4:5

¹ קֶ֖דֶם east ² סֻכָּה hut, shelter ³ צֵל shade

וַיְמַן¹ יְהֹוָה־אֱלֹהִים קִיקָיֹון²

וַיַּעַל ׀ מֵעַל לְיוֹנָה
לִהְיֹות צֵל³ עַל־רֹאשׁוֹ
לְהַצִּיל לֹו מֵרָעָתֹו

וַיִּשְׂמַח יֹונָה עַל־הַקִּיקָיֹון²
שִׂמְחָה⁴ גְדֹולָה:

4:6

מָנָה¹ PI: appoint קִיקָיֹון² castor oil plant צֵל³ shade שִׂמְחָה⁴ joy, happiness

וַיְמַן¹ הָאֱלֹהִים תּוֹלַעַת² בַּעֲלוֹת הַשַּׁחַר³ לַמָּחֳרָת⁴

וַתַּ֥ךְ אֶת־הַקִּֽיקָי֖וֹן⁵

וַיִּיבָֽשׁ:⁶

4:7

¹מָנָה PI: appoint ²תּוֹלַעַת worm ³שַׁחַר dawn ⁴מָחֳרָת the next day ⁵קִיקָיוֹן castor oil plant ⁶יָבֵשׁ Q: dry up, be dry

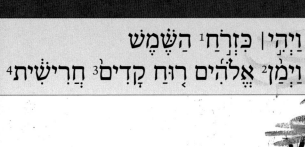

וַיְהִ֣י ׀ כִּזְרֹ֣חַ¹ הַשֶּׁ֗מֶשׁ
וַיְמַ֨ן² אֱלֹהִ֜ים ר֤וּחַ קָדִים֙³ חֲרִישִׁ֔ית⁴

וַתַּ֥ךְ הַשֶּׁ֛מֶשׁ עַל־רֹ֥אשׁ יוֹנָ֖ה
וַיִּתְעַלָּ֑ף⁵

וַיִּשְׁאַ֥ל אֶת־נַפְשׁוֹ֙ לָמ֔וּת

וַיֹּ֕אמֶר

ט֥וֹב מוֹתִ֖י מֵחַיָּֽי׃

4:8

¹זָרַח Q: rise, shine ²מָנָה PI: appoint ³קָדִים east ⁴חֲרִישִׁי stifling ⁵הִתְעַלֵּף HTP: become faint

¹חָרָה Q: become hot, be kindled ²קִיקָיוֹן castor oil plant

חַס Q: pity, be troubled about ²קִיקָיוֹן castor oil plant ³עָמַל Q: toil, work hard

4:11

חָס Q: pity, be troubled about ²רִבּוֹ ten thousand ³שְׂמֹאל left hand, left

Explanations of Select Images

Jonah 1:9 – עִבְרִי אָנֹכִי "I am a Hebrew." עִבְרִי is first used to describe Abram in Gen 14:13, and it is always used with reference to the ethnic people of Israel. We illustrated Jonah at Sinai (an anachronism, admittedly) as the most iconic image of what it meant to belong to Israel.

Jonah 1:11 – מַה־נַּעֲשֶׂה לָּךְ ... כִּי הַיָּם הוֹלֵךְ וְסֹעֵר "'What shall we do to you?' ... because the sea was growing more stormy." In the first speech bubble, we illustrated two possibilities for satisfying divine wrath: tying up Jonah or flogging him. The final Hebrew clause is listed as the narrator's aside (in a grey textbox), but syntactically it could be reported speech.

Jonah 1:14a – אַל־נָא נֹאבְדָה בְּנֶפֶשׁ הָאִישׁ הַזֶּה "Do not let us perish because of the life of this man!" As in Jonah 1:6 and elsewhere, a red "X" indicates negation. The lightning strike and large wave on the left side of the image show a possible way the sailors could have perished.

Jonah 1:14b – וְאַל־תִּתֵּן עָלֵינוּ דָּם נָקִיא ... כַּאֲשֶׁר חָפַצְתָּ עָשִׂיתָ "And do not place (lit. "give") on us innocent blood ... Just as you desired, you have done." The sailors don't want God to hold them accountable for Jonah's death, in case he is innocent after all; hence, the courtroom scene. In the third text box, the sailors describe God as having acted in sovereign freedom with what he desired to do, which is why we portrayed God sending the storm with his hand.

Jonah 2:7 – הָאָרֶץ בְּרִחֶיהָ בַעֲדִי לְעוֹלָם "As for the land, its bars were behind me forever." The word "bars" often refers to what fortifies the city gates to keep people out (e.g. Deut 3:5; 1 Sam 23:7). According to this image, Jonah has tried to get to land, but the land has locked him out.

Jonah 2:9–10a – מְשַׁמְּרִים הַבְלֵי־שָׁוְא חַסְדָּם יַעֲזֹבוּ "The adherents of worthless wisps will forsake their (experience of) steadfast love." Of the many possible interpretations, we believe Jonah, in false piety, refers to the sailors. Jonah says they will return to their idols (cf. 1:5): their sacrifice and vows will be in vain (cf. 1:16), but he will sacrifice with thanksgiving and will fulfill his vow (2:10). See Kevin J. Youngblood, *Jonah* (Grand Rapids, MI: Zondervan, 2013), 112–113.

Jonah 3:9 – וְשָׁב מֵחֲרוֹן אַפּוֹ "And he may return from the burning of his anger." We illustrated this with a fire being extinguished (see also 3:10).

Jonah 4:2b – כִּי אַתָּה אֵל־חַנּוּן וְרַחוּם אֶרֶךְ אַפַּיִם וְרַב־חֶסֶד "Because you are a merciful and tender God, slow to anger and abounding in steadfast love." We illustrated חַנּוּן as a king looking upon the lowly and רַחוּם as a king caring for a baby (רַחוּם is a motherly term; cf. רֶחֶם "womb"). אֶרֶךְ אַפַּיִם literally means "length of nostrils"–it takes a long time to arouse God's anger, illustrated by the near thousand years between the golden calf and the exile/destruction of Jerusalem. God's great covenant-keeping love is pictured as his unmerited favor toward Abraham, Isaac, and Jacob.

Jonah 4:3–4 – וַיֹּאמֶר יהוה הַהֵיטֵב חָרָה לָךְ "And YHWH said, 'Are you thoroughly angry?'" When הֵיטִיב is used as an adverbial infinitive, it means to do something thoroughly (e.g. Deut 9:21; 2 Kgs 11:18). This is confirmed when Jonah affirms that he is thoroughly angry, unto death (4:9).

Hebrew-English Dictionary

This dictionary lists all and only the non-footnoted words in Jonah: verbs with a root occuring 100+ times and non-verbs that occur 100+ times. Glosses are adapted from HALOT.

A code usually precedes the English gloss to specify the part of speech: N = noun, ADJ = adjective, ADV = adverb, PREP = preposition, and PRO = pronoun. After the gloss for each noun, an (m) or (f) specifies gender. Verbs are listed according to their binyan (stem): Q = qal (pa'al), NI = nif'al, PI = pi'el, HI = hif'il, and HTP = hitpa'el.

We reflect a growing movement of professors who require students to memorize all verbs as binyan-specific words in the 3ms qatal form. Verbal meaning resides only in a binyan-specific word, not in an abstract consonantal root. To assist traditional students, we have listed the consonantal root for each non-qal verb, noting the actual word in Jonah.

אֶרֶץ	N: land, earth (f)		**א**
אֲשֶׁר	who, that, which	אָבַד	Q: become lost; perish
אֵת	(marks a definite direct object)	אָדָם	N: man(kind), people (m)
אַתָּה	PRO: you (ms)	אֲדָמָה	N: ground, land (f)
ב		אֶחָד	ADJ: one
בְּ	PREP: in; with; against	אִישׁ	N: man, husband (m)
בָּא	Q: come, enter	אַךְ	but; only, truly
בְּהֵמָה	N: domestic animals (f)	אַל	no, not
בוא	(root consonants of בָּא)	אֶל	PREP: to, towards
בֵּין	PREP: between	אֵל	N: god, God (m)
בֵּן	N: son (m)	אֱלֹהִים	N: god(s), God (m)
בְּעַד	PREP: behind, through; for	אָמַר	Q: say
בָּקָר	N: cattle, herd (m)	אֲנִי	PRO: I
ג		אָנֹכִי	PRO: I
גָּדוֹל	ADJ: big, great	אַף	N: nose; anger (m)
גדל	(root consonants of גִּדֵּל)	אַרְבַּע	N: four

הִתְכַּסָּה	HTP: cover oneself	גִּדֵּל	PI: raise, bring up

ו

וְ	and, also, even; but		

ד

דבר	(root consonants of דָּבָר and דִּבֵּר)
דָּבָר	N: word, matter, thing (m)
דֹּבֵר	Q: (participle only) speak
דִּבֵּר	PI: speak
דָּם	N: blood (m)
דֶּרֶךְ	N: path, way; conduct (f)

ז

זָבַח	Q: slaughter, sacrifice
זֶבַח	N: sacrifice (m)
זֶה	PRO: this
זָכַר	Q: remember

ה

הַ	the
הֲ	(interrogative particle)
הִגִּיד	HI: tell, inform
הוּא	PRO: he, it; that
הוֹסִיף	HI: do again/more
הֵחֵל	HI: begin
הָיָה	Q: be, become; happen
הֵיטִיב	HI: do good; do thoroughly
הִכָּה	HI: strike, smite
הָלַךְ	Q: walk, go
הֶעֱבִיר	HI: send across
הֶעֱלָה	HI: bring up, cause to rise
הִפִּיל	HI: drop, throw down
הִצִּיל	HI: rescue
הַר	N: mountain (m)
הַרְבֵּה	N: many (m); ADV: very, much
הֵשִׁיב	HI: return, bring back
הִשְׁלִיךְ	HI: throw

ח

חַיִּים	N: life, lifetime (m)
חלל	(root consonants of הֵחֵל)
חֶסֶד	N: steadfast love (m)
חשב	(root consonants of חִשֵּׁב)
חִשֵּׁב	PI: compute, think of, plan

ט

טוֹב	ADJ: good, pleasant

י

יָדַע	Q: know
יהוה	N: (God's covenant name) (m)
יוֹם	N: day (m)
יטב	(root consonants of הֵיטִיב)
יָכֹל	Q: be able, capable
יָם	N: sea; west (m)
יָמִין	N: right side, right (m)
יסף	(root consonants of הוֹסִיף)
יָצָא	Q: go out
יָרֵא	Q: fear, be afraid

מְלָאכָה   N: work, occupation (f)

מֶלֶךְ   N: king, ruler (m)

מִן   PREP: from, out of; more than

מַעֲשֶׂה   N: deed, action (m)

מָצָא   Q: find

מֵת   Q: die

נ

נָא   please, surely

נגד   (root consonants of הִגִּיד)

נֶגֶד   PREP: opposite, in front of

נָגַע   Q: touch, reach

נָהָר   N: river, stream (m)

נחם   (root consonants of נִחַם)

נִחַם   NI: regret, relent, be sorry

נכה   (root consonants of הִכָּה)

נפל   (root consonants of הִפִּיל)

נָפַל   Q: fall down

נֶפֶשׁ   N: throat; life, soul (f)

נצל   (root consonants of הִצִּיל)

נָשָׂא   Q: carry; lift up

נִשְׁבַּר   NI: be broken

נָתַן   Q: give

ס

סבב   (root consonants of סָבַב)

סִבֵּב   PI: go around

ע

עבר   (root consonants of הֶעֱבִיר)

יָרַד   Q: go down

יָשַׁב   Q: sit; dwell

כ

כְּ   PREP: as, like; according to

כַּאֲשֶׁר   just as

כִּי   because, that, but, when

כֹּל   N: all, each, every (m)

כְּלִי   N: vessel; implement; weapon (m)

כִּסֵּא   N: chair, throne (m)

כסה   (root consonants of כִּסָּה and הִתְכַּסָּה)

כִּסָּה   PI: cover, conceal

כַּף   N: palm (f)

ל

לְ   PREP: to, for

לֹא   no, not

לֵבָב   N: heart (m)

לָבַשׁ   Q: put on, clothe oneself

לַיְלָה   N: night (m)

לִפְנֵי   PREP: in front of; ADV: before

לָקַח   Q: take, grab

מ

מַה   PRO: what?

מות   (root consonants of מֵת)

מָוֶת   N: death (m)

מִי   PRO: who?

מַיִם   N: water (m)

קָרָא	Q: call, shout
קָרַב	Q: come near, approach

ר

רָאָה	Q: see
רֹאשׁ	N: head (m)
רַב	ADJ: many, much; great
רוּחַ	N: wind; spirit (f)
רַע	Q: be bad, be evil
רַע	ADJ: bad, evil, wicked
רֵעַ	N: friend, neighbor (m)
רָעָה	Q: tend; graze
רָעָה	N: evil, calamity (f)
רעע	(root consonants of רַע)

שׂ

שָׂמַח	Q: be glad, rejoice

שׁ

שֶׁ	who, that, which
שָׁאַל	Q: ask
שבר	(root consonants of נִשְׁבַּר)
שוב	(root consonants of הֵשִׁיב)
שָׁכַב	Q: lie down
שָׁלוֹשׁ	N: three
שלך	(root consonants of הִשְׁלִיךְ)
שלם	(root consonants of שִׁלַּם)
שִׁלַּם	PI: (re)pay, make whole
שָׁם	ADV: there; then, at that time
שָׁמַיִם	N: sky, heaven (m)

עָבַר	Q: pass over, pass by
עַד	PREP: as far as; ADV: while
עוֹד	ADV: again, still, yet
עוֹלָם	N: long time, forever (m)
עָזַב	Q: leave, abandon
עַיִן	N: eye; spring (f)
עִיר	N: city, town (f)
עַל	PREP: on; concerning; against
עַל־כֵּן	therefore
עלה	(root consonants of הֶעֱלָה)
עָלָה	Q: ascend, go up
עַם	N: people (m)
עִם	PREP: with
עָמַד	Q: stand; stop
עָנָה	Q: reply, answer
עָשָׂה	Q: do, make, create
עֶשְׂרֵה	N: teen
עַתָּה	ADV: now

פ

פָּנִים	N: face (f)

צ

צֹאן	N: flock (sheep and goats) (m)

ק

קֹדֶשׁ	N: holiness (m)
קוֹל	N: noise, voice (m)
קום	(root consonants of קָם)
קָם	Q: rise, get up

שְׁנַיִם	N: two		שָׁמַע	Q: hear; listen to, obey
שָׁתָה	Q: drink		שמר	(root consonants of שִׁמֵּר)
			שִׁמֵּר	PI: be follower of, adherent of
ת			שֶׁמֶשׁ	N: sun (f)
תַּחַת	PREP: under; instead of		שֵׁנִי	ADJ: second

MW01256490

Published by GlossaHouse, LLC

GlossaHouse, LLC
110 Callis Circle
Wilmore, KY 40390

Publisher's Cataloging-in-Publication Data

54 pages ; 25.4cm — (HA'ARETS, Picture Hebrew)

ISBN: 978-1942697947

Library of Congress Control Number: 2019953248

Printing in the United States of America

Second printing, 2019

The Hebrew text comprises the entire book of Jonah taken from Biblia Hebraica Stuttgartensia: With Werkgroep Informatica, Vrije Universiteit Morphology; Bible. O.T. Hebrew. Werkgroep Informatica, Vrije Universiteit. Logos Bible Software, 2006.

www.glossahouse.com